Mimi the Complaining Cat

written by
Winsome Bailey

illustrated by
Mel Casipit

Mimi the Complaining Cat

Copyright © 2025

All rights reserved. No part of this publication may be produced, distributed, or transmitted in any form or by any means, including photocopying, recording, or other electronic or mechanical methods, without the prior written permission of the publisher, except in the case of brief quotations embodied in critical reviews and certain other non-commercial uses permitted by copyright law.

Published by Conscious Dreams Publishing
www.consciousdreamspublishing.com

Illustrated by Mel Casipit

Edited by Jackie Raymond

Typeset by Bryony Dick

ISBN: 978-1-917584-21-0

Dedication

I dedicate this book to my loving husband and children, whose patience and unwavering support made this journey possible. Your belief in me gave me the strength to keep going.

I am Mimi, Jenae's cat.

The complaining cat, the 'always appearing out of nowhere' cat.

The 'nothing is ever good enough' cat.

The 'no salmon, no chicken, no duck, not even playing with my stuffed mouse' cat.

Meow, meow, meow!

I enjoy a stroke and a cuddle, as I snuggle on my mum's lap, but sure enough just as I settle, she tells me that's enough.

Meow, meow, meow!

Jenae's mum is calling her; she needs to eat. Her hair needs to be washed. It's homework time. Darn! When will it be my time?

Meow, meow, meow!

Meow, meow, I want my mum.
Meow, meow, I want some food.
Meow, meow, I need my litter changed.
Meow, meow, yes, it's me complaining again!

Meow, meow. Oh, botheration! They've gone and left me: gone on an exploration. But oh, they will wish they had never left me!

Oops! Pooped on her bed.
That will teach her.

       Meow, meow, meow!

Oh, how I wish I could go with them, as I watch them leave wistfully. This is not the first or second time. I wish I had a dime for all the times...

They've gone to church to sing 'Hallelujah!' Then it's off to Grandma's to eat roast potatoes, turkey and gravy.

She makes sure that I am left with plenty of food, and I have my toys to stimulate me all day.

But I would give it all up if she would stay and play.

But evening comes, and my mum returns. My excitement's overflowing. I am never letting her out of my sight again.

Meow, meow, meow!

That does not last long, as she walks away singing a song. Jenae has her doll Fifi in hand. She shoos me away, her friend is here to play. I am left alone; all forlorn.

Meow, meow, meow!

I never want her to leave me again, so a plot I will devise. I will walk with a limp, a hiccup, and a squint, and act as if I am sick.

'Oh, dearie, dearie me,' she says. 'You do not seem well at all, you poor, poor thing. Come, hop on my lap, your favourite song I will sing. Let me get you some milk, some fish, and your toy.'

Meow, meow, meeeooow!

'Jenae! Jenae!' Her friends are calling, and with a gentle nudge I am falling.

I suppose I have to get off her lap.
Oh...! I was hoping to take a nap!

Meow, meow, meow!

My mum Jenae is always busy! They have now gone out to the cinema and for pizza. She doesn't seem to have any time for me. Oh, how I love sitting on her knees!

Thunder is rolling and the lightning flashes. I am feeling frightened, and my fear heightens.

    Meow, meow, meow!

Where are they? Why are they not back home? This noise I cannot abide. I feel so scared, I have to hide.

    Meow, meow, meow!

My mum has been gone for a while. I think I will have a snack. She is always leaving me alone. When will she come back?

Oh, look! The front door has been left open. I think that it is broken. Adventure beckons, and through the door I bolt.

I am not staying here a minute longer. I'm going to explore out yonder. My mum Jenae has never allowed me out before, for fear that I may get lost and wander. She will wish that she had not left me again!

Meow, meow, meow!

Woohoo!!! This is fun, to play with all the bugs, as well as the many hugs that I have had on the way. Perhaps I could find a new mum, now that I have run away.

The sun is out, the thunder has stopped, the lightning has gone away. It's fun to jump, skip and run and explore, as I go along my way. Oh, I'm really having a lot of fun!

Meow, meow, meow!

I met Samantha. She was so nice. She played with me until it was night. 'I have had so much fun with you,' she said. 'Now it's time for me to head home to bed.'

'Can I come home with you?' I begged.

'Oh no, my dear. You must go home instead. Your mummy must be worried. Now scurry home before it gets too dark. Be careful, now. Mr Jim has a dog named Sarki Sark, who roams around with a very loud bark.'

Where has the time flown? All my new friends have gone home, and I am now alone. The sun is no more, instead in its place is the moon. It's time to head home. No more will I roam, as I am hungry, lonely and cold.

Meow, meow, meow!

Oh dear, it's now dark. My way I cannot see. I am not sure how far I will have to walk. It's very eerie! Ooh, I think I am lost!

Meow, meow, meow!

Woof! Woof! Oh dear, what is that sound?
It seems really close to me.
As I look up, huge teeth I see!

Meow, meow, meow!

He is big, with eyes like fire. Oh, my back is up against the wire. Oh, I wish I were standing on something higher, so I wouldn't seem so small!

Meow, meow, meow!

I want my mum! It's no longer fun. I should not have run away. I should have told my mum I was sad whenever she goes away. I would give anything to be back at home with my mum Jenae, my cosy blanket, and a nice fish tray. But home seems so far away!

Meow, meow, meow!

'Mimi! Mimi! Where are you?
Oh my goodness, where are you?'
Jenae called out loud.

'It's all my fault that she's run away!
I should have spent more time with her, not only at nights but during the day.
She needed my time, more cuddles and strokes. After all, she has been leaving me plenty of clues! I promise to listen more to your cues, and include you when I play, rather than send you away.
Mimi, where are you? Where are you?'

Meow, meow, meow!

Phew! I can hear my mum calling. She doesn't sound happy at all!
I wish I hadn't run away, it wasn't the right thing to do.
In future I promise to let my mum know when I am feeling sad and blue.

'Oh, there you are!' my mum said.

'Why did you run away? Do you realise that you've been gone all day?' she said, with tears in her eyes, her arms outstretched.

A smile on her face appeared. 'It's clear that you've been sad. We will play and roll and skip and jump. You can also play with my dad.'

'My darling Mimi, we would never leave you! I will always be back, there's no need to worry. The time will fly in a hurry, so there is no need to get in a flurry!'

My mum Jenae is the best when all is said and done. I would walk a thousand miles for her. She treats me well, so I cannot dwell on the times I am left alone. I am learning to be good and complaining less. I am really trying to do my best.

Meow, meow, meow!

I don't misbehave because I am bad, it's just that I am feeling sad. When I am left, I do not understand if or when you will be back again. Not knowing fills my eyes with tears, and sometimes it is more than I can bear. But now that I know you will be back, I no longer feel anxious and fear.

'Well done, Mimi, such a good cat, Mimi. The place is no longer a mess, no frown on your face, a smile in its place. So happy and playful you are. You are the best cat ever, and I will love you forever.'

Well... until I am left home alone again!

Meow, meow, meow!

THE END

About the Author

Meet Winsome—storyteller, adventurer, and expert at seeing the world through the eyes of a child. After spending years helping kids grow and thrive, she decided to sprinkle some magic into books just for YOU!

Winsome has been writing children's books for six years, filling them with fun, excitement, and just a little bit of mischief. She published her first book in 2021, and she hasn't stopped dreaming up amazing stories since! She loves imagining wild adventures, creating lovable characters, and making learning feel like an exciting journey.

When she's not writing, Winsome is probably daydreaming about her next big story—or maybe even going on a little adventure of her own!

Acknowledgements

A special acknowledgement goes to Jacquelyn Shreeves-Lee, Mecheal Pryce, my fellow authors, Jasmin, Jenae, Reggie, Xavier and, of course, Mimi — without all of you, this would not have been achievable. Thank you from the bottom of my heart.

Finally, I'd like to extend my gratitude to Daniella of Conscious Dreams Publishing, whose passion for beautiful books and exceptional writing is truly inspiring. I was deeply impressed by her dedication to mentoring and supporting new writers. She helps us turn our dreams into reality.

Separation Anxiety

For parents, caregivers, and teachers, this book comes with a guide to separation anxiety:

- What is separation anxiety?
- How can adults help to ease separation anxiety in children they care for?
- ...And prompts to help children better express any anxiety they may feel.

Find this guide at: www.tinyurl.com/Mimithecat

Transforming diverse writers
into successful published authors

Let's connect

www.ingramcontent.com/pod-product-compliance
Lightning Source LLC
Chambersburg PA
CBHW040159100526
44590CB00001B/11